How to Opt Out (not Drop Out) of School

A Guide for Teens for Self-Directed Education

by Lisa Nielsen

an imprint of Eifrig Publishing
Lemont   Berlin

© 2021 by Lisa Nielsen
Printed in the United States of America

All rights reserved. This publication is protected by Copyright, and permission should be obtained from the publisher prior to any prohibited reproduction, storage in a retrieval system, or transmission in any form or by any means, electronic, mechanical, photocopying, recording, or likewise.

Published by Eifrig Publishing,
PO Box 66, Lemont, PA 16851.
Knobelsdorffstr. 44, 14059 Berlin, Germany

For information regarding permission, write to:
Rights and Permissions Department,
Berry Street Books, an imprint of Eifrig Publishing,
PO Box 66, Lemont, PA 16851, USA.
permissions@eifrigpublishing.com, 888-340-6543.

Library of Congress Cataloging-in-Publication Data

Nielsen, Lisa,
  How to Opt Out (Not Drop Out) of School: A Guide for Teens for Self-Directed Education /
by Lisa Nielsen.
     p.   cm.

Paperback ISBN: 978-1-63233-048-2
Ebook ISBN: 978-1-63233-049-9

  1. Education 2. Reform
  I. Nielsen, Lisa, II. Title.

25 24 23 22 2021
5 4 3 2 1

Printed on acid-free paper. ∞

The Innovative Educator Series

Fix the School, Not the Child: 20 Ideas for Parents Who Want to Advocate for the Rights of their Child in School
ISBN 978-1-63233-018-5 ($7.99)

Building a Strong Home-School Connection with Cell Phones (with Willyn Webb)
ISBN 978-1-63233-005-5 ($7.99)

How to Opt Out (Not Drop Out) of School: A Guide for Teens for Self-Directed Education
ISBN 978-1-63233-048-2 ($7.99)

Supporting Student Personal Learning Networks
ISBN 978-1-63233-085-7 ($7.99)

The Uncomfortable History of American Schooling: 1500s -Today
ISBN 978-1-63233-091-8 ($7.99)

The Social Classroom: Engaging Learners with Cell Phones & Social Media
ISBN 978-1-63233-089-5 ($7.99)

The Working Home Educator's Guide to Success: Stories and Advice for Working Families That Want to Home Educate
ISBN 978-1-63233-087-1 ($7.99)

Table of Contents

Introduction
Live and learn your way
It's all a matter of perspective
It's no accident
You didn't know you could opt out
Paper-training and validation
Learning is life. Life is learning.
Why opt out?
Hope is on the horizon and it begins with choice!

Let's Get Started!
A Brief History of Schooling
You're in good company! Successful people who opted out
Know the language
Know the law in your state
Find others who are home educating in your area and online Why opt out? Adult and a teen testimonial
Convincing your parents that opting out is best
What if my parents say no?

Learning without Traditional School
  Online education options
  Alternative Education Options
  Options for consideration before you turn 18
  Opening Educational Resources
  High school equivalency exam
  Attending college without going to high school
  Prepare for college admission

Passions and Portfolios
Exploring, discovering, and pursuing your passions
Building your personal learning network
  Creating a personal success plan
  Developing an ePortfolio

About the Author and Contributors
About the author
About the contributors

Welcome to the start of a new path! You've decided to take control of your own learning and discover your own path to pursuing your passions and achieving success. Whether you take the traditional route or an alternative, it is important that you are aware of the options and empowered to decide what is right for you.

Introduction

You are about to experience something wholly new. It will appear to challenge or even defy much of what you've been taught to believe. While much of the world chants the mantra: finish school (then get a corporate job, open an IRA and retire), this book will encourage you to do just the opposite. The writers of this guide feel that this view of education is worth your consideration. Moreover, we feel the world is ready for it.

Live and learn your way

The idea of opting out of school may seem strange at first. Indeed, to most people, it is strange, because the suggestion blatantly contradicts everything we might believe about the preparations necessary for a successful life. While the initial concern over your fate is quite legitimate, it is important that we begin to understand why we experience that shock – and ask ourselves, "Why are we really here?"

If the answer is 'to learn' then the next natural question should be to ask whether that is being accomplished. In this environment, this school, are we learning? Is there a better way? For most of us the answer is yes – there is a better way. Your way! This is **Freedom in Learning**. It's the freedom to take responsibility for your own learning, experience and life.

Radical and bizarre? Maybe. But this guide will show you that it's not uncommon. In fact, though the memory of the American public is short, historically, compulsory school is truly a new method of learning. We assume that it is the best way for us to learn as we assume it was the best way for our predecessors to learn. Neither may be the case.

This guide will give you the information and encouragement you need to consider what the best education option is for you and you alone. Some of the concepts may challenge what you already believe, so it's very important that we first consider the following key points…

It's all a matter of perspective

Our perception of how the world works is largely due to the way our perception of it has been trained. Most in today's society believe that only by adhering to a very particular institutionalized process allows us to achieve a similarly predetermined success in life. It's very important that we begin to differentiate between what we actually want for our lives and what we've been made to believe we want – having been subject to limited and controlled 'real world' exposure for close to the first two decades of our lives.

The current public school system has trained us for mainstream operations. Through this, we have been unwittingly plugged into an artificial paradigm whereby every facet of our lives has been manufactured to exacting predetermined specifications.

Authentic learning, fundamental logic and reasoning, true inner spirituality and self-exploration are the enemy of these institutions, and where they do actually appear, do so as either rebellions against or a deterioration of the mandated standard. Modern mainstream society labels the notion of organic living, natural learning and independent thought as quaintly alternative and promotes instead a pre-packaged existence as both normal and desirable.

Simply put – we don't know who we are anymore.

A layman's study of the history of American educational systems cannot fail to notice the change wrought by industrialization: a centralizing preference for institutionalized forced-schooling and compulsory pre-selected mass education. Rarely do we wonder who is behind the funding or trajectory of the total system, but when we do investigate we find that it was corporate industrialists, who supported the establishment of federalized, compulsory schooling and funded the politicians dedicated to securing it. John Taylor Gatto[1] traces the etiology of forced schooling and reveals the political and corporate axioms that animate it.

The whole system was built on the premise that isolation from first-hand information and

---
1 www.johntaylorgatto.com/chapters/2b.html

fragmentation of the abstract information presented by teachers would result

in obedient and subordinate graduates, properly respectful of arbitrary orders.

Once this is understood – that the institution of public schooling did not originate from the pure, idealistic pursuit of knowledge; that what we call "education" in fact began with a focus on vocational training for the purpose of the steady supply of employees of a given industry – we are forced to reconsider its effectiveness, and to wonder anew just how it is we best learn.

It's no accident

Ultimately, the details point to a single realization: *Public schooling was never meant to foster intellectual growth.* Quite the contrary.

It was designed to create varying levels of workers to support the rise in industry and perpetuate the bank-owned economy. The work of John Taylor Gatto provides a more detailed understanding of the history of school (for which we refer you to "[I am no longer willing to hurt children](#)."[2]) In the meantime, let us ponder the broad philosophical outlines.

From the time we enter preschool at the tender age of four, we are bombarded with materials, curricula, games and carefully selected language (the very same eventually used to train the themselves in how to teach.) School will aggressively encourage us to select a career based on what the school tells us we are intellectually suited for. Endless, compulsive grading and sorting by level, aptitude and relative age come to resemble fixed product specifications. At the end of the assembly line, we are propelled along toward that general goal where we will fail or succeed in varying degrees to accomplish the tasks for which we were designed. Professionals are separated from blue-collar workers as early as third grade, and twelve to fifteen years later we each graduate with ingrained, disparate roles: lawyers and sanitation workers, artists and cashiers, cops and those whom they will ultimately send to prison.

---

[2] innovativeeducator.com/2011/01/i-am-no-longer-willing-to-hurt-children.html

There is no freedom in this systematic schooling environment. There is no respect for personal choice, and indications otherwise are superficial and illusory, as a cursory glance at the condition of the average American youth suggests. Something is terribly wrong. Teens are plagued with violence, drugs, social status issues, grade and testing stress and more. No wonder they think school sucks. And what's more, the society in which they are bound to register their discontent will respond by inventing corresponding psychiatric conditions and medicating them until pragmatic docility replaces the impulse to rebel.

As a nation, we are sick and we are tired; we are in an economic mess. Perhaps we should rebel. Perhaps we should take responsibility for our own experiences and claim our human freedom once and for all!

The infamous words of Roger Waters exclaimed, "We don't need no education!" I don't think education is the problem though. It's institutionalized schooling that is the problem. Let us understand first that school and education are not, and never were, *synonymous*.

> *De-schooling is not just the child recovering from school damage. It's also the parents exploring their own school and childhood damage and proactively changing their thinking until the paradigm shift happens.*
> ~ *Robyn Coburn*
> *Unschooling Mom, writer, artist & teacher*

You didn't know you could opt out

Of course you didn't know you could opt out! You've been trained to think that the only alternative is a disgraceful and defeated exit. If you're reading this, you are likely to agree that school sucks – and you have been told repeatedly that's how life is. But what if it wasn't?

Here's the good news. You can, quite literally, opt out of this conveyor belt existence. You are allowed the true freedom to discover who you are, what your personal goals and desires are – and what they are not – and then pursue those in the way you choose!

It's important to note that we DON'T NEED TO KNOW what we want to do in order to make the choice to set out on a different path. We've been conditioned for so long to follow orders that when someone decides to leave traditional schooling, they will often need a time of decompression or "deschooling".

Choosing to be free is the first step in claiming the happiness and inspiration that is our birthright. The details of what to do with ourselves will become clear...GUARANTEED! *Have fun learning for the rest of your life!*

Paper-training and validation

If you're among the "paper-trained", like most Americans, you will ask yourself *"what about a diploma or degree?"* This is a natural question. We all grow up believing that we need school because it rewards our compulsory obedience with a diploma. We believe this to be a necessary ingredient to a successful life.

But let us ponder this a moment. Let us ask ourselves why we place such importance on a degree. *Really ponder why.* Find a deeper answer than *"because I can get a better job"*.

We have been trained to be utterly dependent on paper validation... *Why?* Why do we allow this piece of paper – generated by some elusive board of strangers – to validate intelligence or skill? Legal licensing may seem like the obvious response here but as you will read further in the guide, this can be obtained without school. Aside from legal issues, though, paper proof doesn't really matter!

I can't give you a brain, but I can give you a diploma.
~ L. Frank Baum, The Wizard of Oz

It's time for us to stop identifying ourselves with our paper and titles generated by a society that requires most of them simply due to bureaucratic inertia. You may think this is a necessary qualification for ultimate happiness, but you have been duped! We all have. We've been trained to think we are insufficient and need to be validated – we don't! Acknowledge yourself by proclaiming, "I am". *Your existence* – before and behind any subsequent attempt to learn - legitimizes you! The real world for which you are theoretically being prepared will not care about your diploma if you are unable to perform; waving it about will not substitute for the results that a genuine engagement with learning can provide. Since it is a truism that you will be judged by your performance, you owe it to yourself to consider whether that piece of paper really is your ticket to success.

That said, if you still feel it is important to you – not to worry. You can still get a degree or diploma without being locked into a schooling routine – and this guide will show you how. But I urge you to truly consider why it's important to you.

> *We need to separate our identities as people from our university degree. That of course, ultimately means letting our names appear naked on our business cards.*
> *~ Wendy Priesnitz*

Learning is life. Life is learning.

Okay, so you get the bit about the degree... but you may wonder: how can one learn what is necessary without school? The answer to this lies again in perception. Release yourself first from the dogmatic definition of learning and consider what learning actually is. Is it something that must be done to you by someone qualified? Downloaded into you, perhaps? Does one learn critical thinking by memorizing rote details and then regurgitating them onto a paper destined for a shelved circular file? Does one develop a love and appreciation and desire to learn in confined, restrictive and personally oppressive environments? Does one truly have access to *all* available resources when one's exposure is limited to one narrow pre-selected curriculum? Is that learning or is that training? Is that education or is that schooling? How much would we have to forget in order to genuinely learn?

This is the most important concept to absorb when we begin to think about opting out.

We may believe that the only way to learn is to have information told to us by some expert appointed by the same system that duped us into believing we cannot learn any other way. On the contrary however, we all are natural-born autodidacts and remain this way until it's drummed out of us. Human beings are born to learn[3]. That is what we do. Many find that they simply cannot truly appreciate learning and human growth from inside a classroom for 15 or more years. Education is not delivered, inflicted, or imposed. It is offered, received, and, above all, incorporated.

Why opt out?

But is school really so bad? Well, for many of us, yes!

While society has lead us to believe if you feel this way you are lazy, unmotivated, and maybe a bit dull-headed the reality is it is often the exact opposite. Don't accept such labels. They are driven by a system that even by *its own standards* has failed.

[3] innovativeeducator.com/2011/04/aligning-school-to-way-we-were-born-to.html

You've heard the stories. College professors who complain their students come unprepared, after years of dependency learning in high school, to critically think, write, or speak on their own. Businesses complain that today's college graduates are not prepared[4] for the jobs they are expected to do. Classes fostering creativity have been stripped from most high schools and in his famous TED Talk Sir Ken Robinson brilliantly reminds us of how school have killed creativity[5].

As we hear the battle cries for more standards, higher standards, common core standards, the reality is that learning for individual students does not call for one standard way to achieve success.

Colleges know this. Professors have resisted the standards movement. That's why colleges don't test their student body like their K - 12 feeders.

The reality is that the same core subjects are simply not important for everyone. For many

---

4 innovativeeducator.com/2011/03/standardized-tests-dont-prepare.html
5 www.ted.com/talks/ken_robinson_says_schools_kill_creativity.html

of us, it is passion that can successfully drive learning. By allowing ourselves to be blindly led down someone else's path, we are becoming statistically dumber than at any point before in history.

Something needs to change and someone needs to change it. That someone is you!

How? By embracing your opportunity to choose. It's time for something new, and it's up to the youth of our world to begin spinning a new wheel!

Hope is on the horizon and it begins with choice!

Beauty, honesty, love for one another... economic stability, physical and emotional health... all blossom when humanity knows and honors the unique talents and passions of all individuals, in ways that contribute to the health of a shared world.

The more society sees the benefits of unplugging from this system, the more improvements we will enjoy in our world and environment. Thanks in part to the internet, which has democratized information access; and social media, which has had an unparalleled effect on collaboration, these are ideas are gaining some serious momentum. These trends suggest that a mass exodus from schooling as it has traditionally been known is in the offing. In fact, as more and more of you – our nation's youth – begin to see that the world outside the classroom has so much more to offer, we all continue to learn and grow and explore.

Learning is not limited to an age, a time, a space or a curriculum – and that is exactly the point!

So this is for you – for the bright, young beautiful souls with a burning desire to experience the rich wonder of the real world NOW and not at some vague time after graduation when you live in the "real world." This is for you – starving to embrace control over your own decisions, your own passions and take charge of what you learn, how you learn and from whom you learn it!

Freedom of choice – you already have it! Embrace it! Use it!

~ Laurette Lynn
Homeschooling Mom
Public speaking and communications expert
Author: <u>Don't Do Drugs and Stay Out of School</u>
(<u>www.unpluggedmom.com/book/</u>)
Website: <u>www.laurettelynn.com</u>

Let's Get Started!

The fact is that given the challenges we face, education doesn't need to be reformed – it needs to be transformed. The key to this transformation is not to standardize education, but to personalize it, to build achievement on discovering the individual talents of each child, to put students in an environment where they want to learn and where they can naturally discover their true passions.

~ Sir Ken Robinson,
The Element: How Finding Your
Passion Changes Everything

A Brief History of Schooling

People didn't always have to go to high school to be successful. Before the relatively recent days of academic inflation, we had professionals who achieved great success without it: medical professionals, lawyers, politicians, teachers and more.

You may have also noticed that people seemed to have achieved success at much earlier ages than they do today. For most of the nineteenth century many states did not require young people to go to school. This changed in the 20th century. By 1918, every state required students to complete schooling up to the elementary level. After that teenagers often spent time integrating into society. Some might be learning a trade, others the family business. Some might follow a pursuit of writing or singing, some became entrepreneurs, others explorers. Some became interested in politics and for some of the academically minded, they would continue their studies, though there were geniuses like Einstein who found school so confining that they simply left.

It wasn't until the turn of the twentieth century that the minimum age of compulsory attendance[6] was raised. As John Taylor Gatto[7] explains, this was in part an attempt to keep the young out of the workforce and in part to create a consumer society. However, before they were forced to stay in school until their late teens, (16 in most states), the younger generation had no trouble in the "real world." Today, if you don't choose to graduate high school, you are stigmatized as a drop-out, and a whole nation worries about you.

6 www.youtube.com/watch?v=uexMYBkfCic
7 en.wikipedia.org/wiki/John_Taylor_Gatto

Currently, about 1/5 of our nation's students drop out of public high schools according to the National Center for Education Statistics[8]. In large urban areas dropout rates reach as high as 50%. Clearly something is not right.

Schools are providing a service that many no longer want, and even those who endure share they are unsatisfied. According to the U.S. Department of Education, students drop out of school for reasons including:

- Dislike of school
- Low academic achievement
- Retention at grade level
- A sense that teachers and administrators do not care about students
- Inability to feel comfortable in a large, depersonalized school setting

Some of the most successful students by standard measures (search "valedictorian[9] Erica Goldson" at Innovativeeducator.com) weren't happy with their high school education. Unfor-

---

8 nces.ed.gov/programs/coe/indicator_coi.asp
9 innovativeeducator.com/2010/09/valedictorian-asks-is-that-all-there-is.html?spref=tw

tunately, many students don't realize that they don't have to go to high school and they don't have to drop out. Instead they can opt out and head straight to an apprenticeship, career, or attend college without completing high school[10] (search "college without high school" at InnovativeEducator.com).

If it seems everyone you know touts the importance of a high school diploma, it may comfort you to know that there are many successful people who did not take that path. In the next section you will learn about some of them.

You're in good company!
Successful people who opted out

It is nothing short of a miracle that modern methods of instruction have not yet entirely strangled the holy curiosity of inquiry.

~ *Albert Einstein*

If you're thinking high school isn't right for you, you're not alone! Below are just a few of the many successful people listed in the Dropouts Hall of Fame[11] who left high school to move on

---

10 t.co/spo7PEt

11 www.collegedropoutshalloffame.com/s.htm

to successful lives. In some cases, students who liked learning, just not the compulsory nature of traditional school, skipped high school and went straight to college.

As Rylie Vandersol who started college at 14 reminds us, "You don't have to be a genius for that to happen." You can search her name at InnovativeEducator.com to learn how she did it.

I suppose it is because nearly all children go to school nowadays and have things arranged for them that they seem so forlornly unable to produce their own ideas.
~ Agatha Christie

Here are some well-known people who choose various careers who choose not to take the traditional path of school to achieve success.

Writers
- **Jane Austen**, novelist. She left school at the age of 11.
- **William Shakespeare**, playwright, poet. Only a few years of formal schooling.
- **Mark Twain,** printer, riverboat pilot, prospector, newspaper reporter, humorist,

author of the first great American novel, *The Adventures of Huckleberry Finn*. Left school in fifth grade.

Entrepreneurs
- **Walt Disney**, producer, director, screenwriter, animator, developer of Disneyland and Disneyworld.
- **Lucille Ball**, actress, comedienne, producer. Co-founder of Desilu Studios. Later bought out her husband's share to become the first woman to own and run a production studio.
- **Andrew Carnegie**, industrialist and philanthropist. Elementary school dropout. Started work at the age of 13 as a bobbin boy in a textile mill. One of the first mega-billionaires in the U.S.

Performers
- **Christina Aguilera**, singer, songwriter.
- **Mary J. Blige**, Grammy-winning singer, songwriter, record producer, and actress.
- **Patrick Stewart**, actor, producer, director, writer.

Presidents

- **Abraham Lincoln**, lawyer, U.S. president. Finished barely a year of formal schooling. He self-taught himself trigonometry (for his work as a surveyor) and read Blackstone on his own to become a lawyer.
- **George Washington**, U.S. president, general, plantation owner. Ended his education after a few years of elementary school.
- **Luiz Inacio Lula da Silva**, Brazilian president. With a fifth grade education only, he shined shoes on the streets of Sao Paulo as a kid but later became a steelworker union leader.

Public Servants

- **Mary Lyon**, education pioneer, teacher, founder of Mount Holyoke College (America's first women's college). Dropped out of high school. Started teaching at the age of 17.
- **Cathy Lanier**, Chief of Police of Washington, DC. Pregnant at 14 she opted out of high school.
- **Florence Nightingale**, founder of modern nursing. Her insistence on sanitary conditions saved many soldiers from death and

otherwise crippling injuries during the Crimean War. No formal education.

Athletes

- **Yogi Berra**, baseball player, coach, and manager. Quit school in the eighth grade.
- **Andre Agassi**, tennis player, winner of 8 Grand Slam titles. Quit school in the ninth grade and turned tennis pro at the age of 16. His father would say he was driving the kids to school but, instead, actually took them to local tennis courts to practice.
- **Mario Andretti**, race-car driver, author.

Science and Exploration

- **Albert Einstein**, Nobel prize-winning physicist, discoverer of the General and Special Theories of Relativity. He left school at 15.
- **Christopher Columbus**, explorer, credited for discovering America. Little formal education.
- **Benjamin Franklin**, inventor, scientist, inventor, diplomat, author, printer, publisher, politician, patriot, signer of the U.S. Declaration of Independence. Dropped out of

Boston Latin. Home schooled with less than two years of formal education.

Everybody is a genius. But if you judge a fish by its ability to climb a tree, it will spend its whole life believing that it is stupid.

~ Albert Einstein

It's important to understand that schooling is not an automatic springboard for success. On the contrary, with the rise in mandatory schooling over the last century, academic success appears to be a whole lot less common than before compulsory schooling.

Compulsory schooling and personal success almost seem mutually exclusive; the first does not automatically bring on the latter, despite what we've been conditioned to believe. Personal success depends on an individual's unique talents, the ability to do real-world work that is meaningful, to think outside the box, and more. These qualities don't produce the higher test scores by which students are measured and school funding is secured; indeed, the current system reliably suffocates them.

More and more often, innovative companies such as Google are acknowledging that academic success is irrelevant. In his New York Times interview with Thomas Friedman, Laszlo Bock, the senior vice president of people operations for Google shared that "G.P.A.'s are worthless as a criteria for hiring, and test scores are worthless. ... We found that they don't predict anything." He also noted that the "proportion of people without any college education at Google has increased over time."

If GPAs, test scores, and even college are not all that important to a company like Google, then what is needed?

Ambition, willingness to keep learning, ownership of the work, leadership, and a fierce tenacity to press forward! None of which are going to have room to blossom fully if we are instead focused on passing exams to simply hang a degree on our wall.

It's time to reconsider the idea that school is the golden ticket to success. It simply is not.

If you feel that you can enrich your experience and achieve your goals without it, then do it! Keep reading to find out how.

Know the Language

High thoughts must have high language.
~ Aristophanes

Opting out of high school is not "dropping out." Learning happens in people, not places. For the purpose of this guide we often use the more common term "homeschooling" as an umbrella term, but there are a variety of practices consistent with this approach. Because more and more families nowadays are 'opting out' of school, the homeschooling option has become increasingly popular. Due to the rich variety of families who enjoy the personalized philosophical freedom of independent education, several different 'styles' of home education have emerged, and thus terms for those varying styles.

Homeschooling, or Home Learning

Homeschooling is the umbrella term for many types of alternatives to traditional school. Homeschooling refers to the education of children outside the school system, often by parents but sometimes by experts with whom students or parents have connected, or tutors. Although prior to the introduction of compulsory school attendance laws, most childhood education occurred within the family or community, homeschooling in the modern sense is an alternative in developed countries to private schools outside the home or educational institutions operated by civil governments.

Homeschooling is a legal option for parents in all fifty states. Parents cite numerous reasons why they homeschool. While the most common reason was once religion, today that reason is cited in less than 20% of all home educating families. Among the other reasons are: wanting to escape an unhealthy schooling environment; desiring better academic results; wanting flexible schedules and ability to travel; wanting improved character/ morality development; more affordable than private education; and philosophical objections to what is taught (i.e. Common Core Standards) or done (i.e. over-testing) in school.

The homeschooling movement began to gain momentum in the 1970's and became a choice for families everywhere. The U.S. Department of Education's National Center for Education Statistics indicates that 3.4% of children are homeschooled in America. To put this into perspective, it is about the same percentage as the number of children who attend charter schools and about 1/3 of the number of children who attend private schools.

To follow are descriptions of various types of homeschooling:

Roadschooling/Worldschooling
Roadschooling is what happens when families hit the road with their children to learn through life on the road. Some do this in RVs, others bikes, others by foot. The mode of transportation is not important. The importance comes from the adventure that happen when

you take learning on the road. Many such families have set up blogs for others to follow their adventures and learning. The <u>Families on The Road</u>[12] site is a hub for such families to share and connect.

Unschooling, Radical Unschooling
(Source: Idzie Desmarais an unschooled adult who blogs at <u>I'm Unschooled. Yes, I can write.</u>[13])

Below are some ways unschooling is defined.

1. Unschooling (usually considered a type of homeschooling) is student-directed learning, which means the child or teen learns whatever they want, whenever they want. Learning is entirely interest driven, not dictated or directed by an external curriculum, by teachers, or by parents. For an unschooler, life is their classroom.

2. Unschooling requires a paradigm shift, one in which you must stop dividing the world into series of occurrences/resources/experienc-

---

12 www.familiesontheroad.com
13 yes-i-can-write.blogspot.com/p/new-to-this-blog-new-to-unschooling.html

es etc. that can be learned from and a series that can not. The world doesn't divide neatly into different subjects and you can't tell right from the outset what a seemingly unimportant question, interest, or TV show obsession will lead to. I learn from: wandering, wondering, listening, reading, watching, discussing, running, writing, daydreaming, searching, researching, meditating, hibernating, playing, creating, growing, doing, helping, and everything else that comprises the day to day happenings of my life.

3. Unschooling, at its heart, is the realization that life and learning are not two separate things. And when you realize that living and learning are inseparable, it all starts to truly make sense.

Natural Learning
Natural learning fosters learning-on-demand where children pursue knowledge based on their interests and parents take an active part in facilitating activities and experiences conducive to learning, but do not rely heavily on textbooks or spend much time teaching, looking instead

for learning opportunities throughout their daily activities. Parents see their role as that of affirming through positive feedback and modeling the necessary skills, and the child's role as being responsible for asking and learning. Both unschooling and natural learning advocates believe that children learn best by doing; a child may learn math skills by operating a small business or sharing in family finances. They may learn animal husbandry keeping dairy goats or meat rabbits, botany tending a kitchen garden, chemistry to understand the operation of firearms or the internal combustion engine, or politics and local history by following a local zoning dispute.

While any type of homeschoolers may also use these methods, the unschooled child initiates these learning activities. The natural learner participates with parents and others in learning together. Knowing the type of education you are pursuing and the different terms used to define it is helpful. Even more important is knowing what the law permits where you live.

> GREAT SECRET: Whenever I'm learning something difficult, I keep expectations low, and aspirations high.
>
> ~*James Marcus Bach*
>
> *Author of "Secrets of a Buccaneer Scholar: How Self-Education and the Pursuit of Passion Can Lead to a Lifetime of Success"*

Know the Law in Your State

Home educators have fought for the right of parents and their children to be educated in the way they feel is best. Over the course of many court cases, a solid foundation has been put in place to provide educational choice for parents and their children. This is an ongoing battle, but as more and more home-educated adults tell their stories, the idea is not only gaining popularity, it is gaining credibility. At the moment, each state has a different set of laws that must be followed. Make sure you know the laws and requirements where you live.

Home-educating families should become actively involved in support of legislation to further protect the individual liberty to educate independently and without oversight by a school board. There are home education advocates who can help you find out more about how you can claim your right to educate yourself freely, when you are ready.

To find out more, visit the home schooling legal defense association[14] website. There you can find a summary of legal options in every state by visiting the State Laws link.[15] You can also find out what public school services you are entitled to.

Find others who are home educating in your area and online

You are not alone. There are other teens pursuing non-schooling options. Find out who they are. They may be willing to share their guidance and expertise. The home schooling legal defense association has put together a resource with both national homeschooling organizations as well as a state-by-state listing.

---

14 www.hslda.org
15 www.hslda.org/laws/default.asp?

There is a vibrant community of homeschoolers online. From discussion boards to blogs, you can connect with other homeschoolers ready to help you enjoy life without school in no time. You can start with the Homeschooling/Unschooling Facebook[16] group affiliated with this guide for a large community of those pursuing life without school for their families. This group is not only supportive of teens who are considering school alternatives, but it is a terrific community to invite your parents to. In the group they'll come across thousands of parents who are enjoying success for their children who do not attend school.

You may also want to learn about the success of grown homeschoolers beyond those who are famous. They're telling their stories and they want others to know about this option. You can start searching InnovativeEducator.com for "profiles of adults who didn't go to school." There you'll read about regular people who grew up without school and learn what they are doing today. When you begin connect-

---

16 www.facebook.com/groups/homeschoolingunschooling

ing with others who were home educated, you'll find there are many legitimate reasons school just didn't work for them.

In this next section, you'll learn why two of the contributors to this guide made the choice to opt out of school as teens.

Why opt out? Teen and adult testimonials

I have never let school interfere with my education.
~ Mark Twain

In a world where being a teen is practically defined by school attendance, making the decision to opt out can be very difficult. After all, this is an age when most adolescents are trying to fit in. Additionally, most people perceive students who leave school as lazy, unmotivated, not bright, etc. Students who have taken charge of their learning know this is not true, but the reality is that they will spend a lot of time convincing others of this.

To follow are the stories of Leah Miller, a teenage girl, and Deven Black, an adult male, at the time of this writing. They share how they grappled with, and then came to the decision, to opt out of high school to acquire an education that suited them best.

As a school principal I have one job and that is to expose kids to a whole lot of different things and help them to get their light bulb to go on.

~ Barbara Slatin, Principal[17]

Leah Miller: School was dimming my bright light

I am an unusual case. I hope one day, what I did will be commonplace, but with my circumstances, for now, I remain unusual. I have always been a "good student." I got straight A's, I did my homework without being bribed, I actually enjoyed going to class most days.

I left school because my inner light was slowly, but surely, being dimmed. I started dreading school and losing all my motivation for the mundane daily homework I was assigned. It was hell to put myself through the day-to-day activities that I didn't care a whit about.

---

17 *Search Barbara Slatin at InnovativeEducator.com to read more*

Fortunately, my mom had a great conversation with a friend that led to a discussion about unschooling--the friend had unschooled his three kids. My mom brought it up to me that night and the seed was planted. She didn't have any agenda when she told me, but as the idea grew inside me, she saw me open like a flower in the desert finally getting water. We talked to that family as we were deciding to leave. They have become a real support system for me.

I left my high school just a few weeks after the initial conversation. My mind was made up, my heart followed and the rest is history. In the beginning, my dad was reluctant and unsure if it was a good decision. To help ease his mind I made a PowerPoint presentation (which you can view by searching Leah Miler at InnovativeEducator.com). You can see the cover below.

By Leah Miller

Then I scheduled a meeting with my parents to help convince them. I took charge of my life and ownership of my learning and left high school right then and there. It was freeing, but also scary.

I got a lot of different reactions when I first left. I am still dealing with the repercussions. Some of my friends and family were very supportive. They saw how much better I was doing. Quite a few of my friends still suffering through the school system were jealous. However, quite a few people dear to me were really upset by my decision. I got angry letters and anonymous hate comments on my <u>blog</u>[18]. Unfortunately, I have kind of grown apart from most of my school friends. Thankfully, I had some really close friends from acting school whom I remain super close with.

It was hard to deal with all of the various responses, but I feel that I have learned a lot and grown as a person from this experience. One of the questions I hear all the time is "So, what do you do all day?" I hate this question. I know that people are just curious and they have every right to want to know more about my unconventional lifestyle. However, that question makes me curl up inside and get that dread feeling in my gut. Sometimes I feel like I am inadequate with what I am doing, but most of the time, I just know that the person asking won't understand the way I live my life, because society hasn't <u>caught up with this</u> growing education revolution yet.

18 leahmiller.typepad.com

I live my life day by day. I take every opportunity I can to learn from life. I believe I am more prepared for life now than when I was still in the sheltered school environment. I have learned how to handle myself efficiently in real-world situations.

I hope to get a job soon. Until then, I do lots of internships with different theaters. Because I have so much free time during the school year, I am really interested in travel. I am going to New York soon for over two weeks to explore and soak in the city. I know that I will learn bucket loads from that trip. I plan to apply to Santa Monica College in the fall and take whatever classes I find interesting. After two years, it is really easy to transfer to a traditional four-year campus school. I passed the California High School Proficiency Exam, the California equivalent of a GED for minors. I am thriving as I live my life the way I want to, without having a "formal education" thrust upon me. I am confident that my path will lead to an amazing future, and I can't wait![19]

---

19 Update: In 2014 Leah entered New York University as a full-time student.

Deven Black: The City was My Classroom

As I think about my own experience decades ago deciding high school was not the place for me I wonder whether anyone, anyplace other than where I was, could have done what I did as successfully at that time. And I think how much easier it would be now.

I grew up in Manhattan and in late 1967, when I left school for the first time at age 14, Manhattan was, for me, a 12 mile long, 1.5 mile wide educational experience. A brief subway or bus ride could deliver me to any one of dozens of museums of art, natural history, craft or occupation. Or I would emerge from underground into what seemed like a different city where the people spoke Chinese, Italian, Spanish or Ukrainian and the food in the restaurants were the best kind of spoon-fed learning.

Eugene McCarthy was emboldening and enlisting young people to become the driving force behind his idealistic campaign for the Presidency and against the Vietnam War. I had already worked on some political campaigns and, when the cold January winds blew the NYC campaign headquarters at Columbus Circle became my second home; second even though I spent more time there than at my family's apartment where I went only to sleep and shower.

New York City was made for the learner and I suspect it was only because I was there that I could realize in retrospect that going to classes at my two high schools, one considered at that time one of the two or three best in the nation, actually interfered with my learning. I'm not sure, but I suspect that had I been living in Oklahoma, Iowa, Arizona or suburban Connecticut my experience would have been radically different.

It would also be radically different today because, thanks to the Internet, and all the wonderful tools that have become available because of it, a fifteen-year-old in Kansas, Kankakee or Kalamazoo could explore even more of the world from their bedroom than I could from the heart of the world when I was fifteen. It is truly an amazing thing that today anyone, almost anywhere, can learn almost anything he or she might want to know about, almost immediately and mostly for free. They would not even have to pay the subway fare I had to fork over.

There is, of course, a qualitative and experiential difference between looking at a picture of a pirogi and popping one in one's mouth, or walking the streets on foot instead of through Google Earth, but one learns what one can the way one has available.

I am not arguing that the average, or even the exceptional, teen has the ability to learn anything on their own or that they would even realize what they might be able to learn. This learning happens best with people like the guides, mentors, interlocutors and others I found to steer me, challenge me, and teach me. I relied on those around me, but today those people can be accessed anywhere in the world via the internet.

School does not work for everyone, but neither does leaving it. We each have our individual paths. Still, if one is not finding beneficial what they are learning in school and they are willing to take the risk and make the effort, the opportunity to get a broader, deeper and more interesting education is richer now than it has even been.

And that is a magnificent thing.

Convincing your parents that opting out is best

Every day I went to school was a constant attack on my self-worth. I learned not to believe in myself. It was a bombardment from all directions; the teachers were saying how bad I was doing in their classes, my family was ashamed of my grades, and the students were attacking me about everything under the sun! I was like a plant trying to grow in darkness--it doesn't. It all left me afraid to dream my dreams-afraid to be my true self! Who wants to show their true self if they're just going to get a rock hurled at it?! The real question is: how do we undo the damage done? We have to take time to dream again, not other peoples', but our own precious dreams that mean everything to us. Our dreams are our life maps.

~ unschooler Jenny Smith

Traditional school is not the best option for personal success for some people...*and that's okay.* However, your parents may see things differently. Parents often expect their children to be raised the way they were. That means going to school. They may not even know there are other options available. That's where you come in. You will need to educate and convince your parents that this is a good choice. You can start by mentioning some of the famous people mentioned earlier who opted out of school. You might want to research them and find out the stories of how school was holding them back.

Sir Ken Robinson's book, *"The Element: How Finding Your Passion Changes Everything,"* has some powerful stories about successful adults who found themselves held back by school. He also has a great video you may want to share with parents about how schools kill creativity. Visit his website[20] for more information.

Peter Gray is another great resource. He is a research professor and author of the book *Free to Learn.* His research and writing focus on children's

---

[20] sirkenrobinson.com

natural ways of learning and the life-long value of play. His <u>Freedom to Learn</u>[21] blog is a terrific resource that looks at the similarities between school and prison, explores how children can learn to read without school, and provides success stories of adults who grew up without school.

After making your case with connections and success stories of others who were home educated, you'll find there are many ideas in this guide to help in your endeavor. You'll find the knowledge you need to begin making your case for opting out of school and opting in to either online learning, an alternative education setting, or learning at home. Regardless of which option you choose, you want your parents to know this is a well-thought out decision.

One way you can do this is by creating a personal success plan and developing an ePortfolio where you will place all of your accomplishments. Both are explained later in this guide and are terrific resources regardless of the <u>learning option</u> you select.

---

21 www.psychologytoday.com/blog/freedom-learn

It is important to be sensitive to how shocking the idea of leaving school will be to most people, especially your parents. As with any successful communication, try to stand in their shoes and see the world through their eyes. Like most people, they have been conditioned their entire lives to believe that doing well in school is the only way to be successful in life. The flip side is that if you don't do well in school, you're likely to be a failure. This perception of how the world works can elicit incredible anxiety when discussing the subject of opting out.

Many parents (and subsequently many kids) believe that the road to success starts in preschool! If you don't get into the right preschool, you won't get into the right elementary school. From there you certainly won't get into the right middle and high school...and college? Forget it, there's no hope. Your life is an avalanche of failure, begun when you tipped the first snowball by not getting into that preschool that the "Best Of" lists recommended. Leaving school means your life is doomed to failure.

Sound familiar? As absurd as this is, even for those who have chosen alternative paths, this voice of fear still may linger in the recesses of one's mind. As you imagine your path to freedom and try to discuss it with others, it is essential to be aware of how this underlying fear may be influencing your thoughts and decisions as well as those to whom you are speaking.

Deschooling

> *Don't expect right now to feel smooth. The days spent in school are like living with a broken leg. The days when unschooling runs smoothly are like living with two strong legs. But the deschooling phase between them is like living with a cast while the leg heals. It won't be as bad as school but won't be as smooth as unschooling.*
>
> *~ Joyce Fetteroll[22] unschooling mom, writer, artist*

Although deschooling may be used to indicate an anti-"institutional school" philosophy, for our purposes, we're referring to a period of time or form of deprogramming for those who have previously been schooled. After so many years of being told what to do, of following schedules handed to you,

---
[22] www.sandradodd.com/joycefetteroll

of pursuing predetermined programs, a good break may be the most important and useful thing for your first steps outside of the educational system. The feeling of exhilaration of the last day of school before summer vacation is what we're looking for, but this time it's bigger and better because it's now about choosing your freedom.

It will be tempting to get busy quickly and many people may suggest structure so that you don't "waste time." Nevertheless, time to be quiet or do nothing so that you can find the voice that guides you is often exactly what you need. There is no rush. As hard as it may be for you (and even more so for parents) to embrace, you are on your own schedule and there are no predetermined ways for your learning to unfold.

Listen again to high school opt out Leah Miller:

"My mom and I were on the same page from the beginning, but my dad needed a little convincing in the first stages. He has come a long way since then, and I appreciate his journey. When I first got the idea to leave school, I grabbed my laptop and opened up Powerpoint. Once I started thinking in detail, the

words and ideas kept flowing from my fingers onto each slide. Many of my ideas and some of my philosophy have changed since then, but it was still a great place to start and a terrific way to solidify my thinking. Creating a <u>presentation</u>[23] for parents and others can be powerful. You can view and download mine. I hope it will be an inspiration and starting point for others who want to do the same."

What if my parents say no?

Sometimes it's possible to persuade parents over time. Other times it is not and students are forced to remain in school, even though they don't want to be there. You can find support and information from students who are also stuck in school, and those who have made it out <u>here</u>[24].

You might find it helpful to talk to a third party who can get to know your situation and even talk to your parents with you. It may also take quite a bit of persistence over time. Find out what your parents care about and research options that meet your needs and address your parents concerns.

---

23 tinyurl.com/sampleoptoutpresentation

24 school-survival.net

In some cases, what it comes down to is that parents basically want someone else to manage their kid's education. If not school, then what? One option is to combine homeschooling with a program like the Liberated Learners model which was first developed at North Star Self-Directed Teens. These programs combine unschooling with having a learning advisor and support for your learning. They also offer a place to go, usually part-time, to interact face-to-face with other learners.

If your parents are willing to homeschool you but don't have the time to work with you, the Catalyst Learning Network[25] is an online network that provides support and direction to your learning. Catalyst develops a learning plan in collaboration with you and your parents, connects you with teachers and mentors in your chosen areas of learning, and helps you find appropriate classes and develop projects. Catalyst will also help you talk to your parents about out-of-school learning options.

---

25 catalystlearning.net

Learning without Traditional School

School has a familiar and unmovable position in our public consciousness, but it is just one of many options. In this section, we'll explore some ways young people are learning and preparing for success without school.

Online education options

"We socialize. It's fun. Socialization, on the other hand, that's where someone trains you how to behave in an institutional setting. Not fun.

~ Sara McGrath,
home education author

There are many reasons a teen may feel school isn't right. For some it might just be about the limitations that exist in a traditional school setting. The following list from teenagers provides a collection of reasons about why they prefer to attend school online:[26]

26 Search "Prefer Online" at InnovativeEducator.com

1. *I can pursue my passions.*
2. *I can focus on my work without distractions from my classmates.*
3. *I can move at my own pace.*
4. *I can sleep in.*
5. *I don't have to compete to share my thoughts and ideas.*
6. *I can take more interesting classes.*
7. *I can learn with a schedule that meets my needs.*
8. *I can learn despite health issues that might get in the way of a traditional class setting.*
9. *I can easily communicate with my teacher when I need to.*
10. *I can easily communicate with my classmates whenever I want.*
11. *I can work ahead if I'm able to.*
12. *I get nearly instant responses from my teachers.*
13. *I get personalized support when I need it.*
14. *I can do all my math for the week on one day if I want to.*
15. *I know how I'm doing, my grades are right on the screen.*
16. *My teachers are just as excited about online learning as I am.*
17. *My parents can see my work and grades.*
18. *My courses are more challenging.*
19. *I can keep up with my work when my family travels.*
20. *I can work around a busy schedule.*

If any of these ideas are appealing, online learning may be a sensible choice for you. In case you were wondering, most online schools are public school programs supported by tax dollars. That means you don't have to pay for it.

The International Association of Online Learning[27] (iNacol) is an association that represents a diverse cross-section of K-12. They can be your start for information about online learning. They also are a source to point you toward providers. This is a way to find a provider [28] in your state.

Alternative Education Options

A true bubble is when something is overvalued and intensely believed. Education may be the only thing people still believe in in America. To question education is really dangerous. It is the absolute taboo. It's like telling the world there's no Santa Claus.
~ Peter Thiel, co-founder of PayPal

---

[27] www.inacol.org

[28] www.inacol.org/resources/faqs/#findol

If you know school is just not right for you, the problem might not be school itself but rather the type of school you are attending. There are alternative school models that honor the passion-driven learning that dedicated teachers and parents value and students deserve.

Here are some models:

Schoolwide Enrichment Model

The Schoolwide Enrichment Model (SEM) provides enriched learning experiences and higher learning standards for all children through three goals: developing talents in all children, providing a broad range of advanced-level enrichment experiences for all students, and providing advanced follow-up opportunities for young people based on their strengths and interests. The SEM focuses on enrichment for all students through high levels of engagement and the use of enjoyable and challenging learning experiences that are constructed around students' interests, learning styles, and preferred modes of expression.

- For an overview of this model of learning search InnovativeEducator.com for <u>Preparing Students for Success by Helping Them Discover and Develop Their Passions.</u>[29]
- For a profile of a school following this model search InnovativeEducator.com for <u>The Island School</u>.[30]
- For a profile of a student who has attended such a school search InnovativeEducator.com for <u>Armond McFadden</u>.[31]
- Here is a <u>Directory of SEM schools</u>.[32]

Democratic Schools

Another popular alternative model is known as democratic schools or free schools. A democratic education employs a theory of learning and school governance where students and staff participate freely and equally in a school democracy. In a democratic school, there is typically shared decision-making among students and staff on matters concerning living, working, and learning together.

---

29 innovativeeducator.com/2010/12/preparing-students-for-success-by.html
30 innovativeeducator.com/2008/12/you-can-get-dalton-education-at-nyc.html
31 innovativeeducator.com/2011/01/profile-of-passion-driven-student.html
31 www.gifted.uconn.edu/sem/semhpage.html

At these schools students decide what to do with their time, and learn as a by-product of the experiences they choose rather than through classes or a standard curriculum. Students have complete responsibility for their education and the school is run by a direct democracy in which students and staff have an equal vote.

You can find a list of schools by searching Democratic schools[33] on Wikipedia. You can watch this video to see what a Democratic school looks like here.[34] You can also read more by searching InnovativeEducator.com for Hey Teacher! Leave Us Kids Alone!!![35] *Alternatives to School* is a comprehensive site about the problems of public education and the advantages to finding alternatives. They have listings of community learning centers, democratic schools, and self-directed learning centers.
alternativestoschool.com

---

33 en.wikipedia.org/wiki/List_of_democratic_schools
33 youtu.be/awOAmTaZ4XI.
33 innovativeeducator.com/2011/01/hey-teacher-leave-us-kids-alone-theres.html

Big Picture Learning Schools:

www.bigpicture.org

Big Picture Learning schools have a mission is to lead vital changes in education, both in the United States and internationally, by generating and sustaining innovative, personalized schools that work in tandem with the real world of the greater community. They believe that in order to sustain successful schools where authentic and relevant learning takes place, we must continually innovate techniques and test learning tools to make our schools better and more rigorous. They believe that in order to create and influence the schools of the future, we must use the lessons learned through our practice and research to give us added leverage to impact changes in public policy. Here is a list of Big Picture Schools.[36]

EdVisions Schools:

www.edvisions.com

EdVisions Schools is a non-profit educational development organization affiliated with the EdVisions Cooperative, the first public school teacher cooperative in the nation. EdVisions

---

36 www.bigpicture.org/category/schools

Schools help create and sustain a network of small, innovative high schools across the U.S. using the EdVisions Model, which consists of these essentials: small learning community, self-directed project based learning, authentic assessment, teacher-ownership. Their innovative teaching model, emphasizes real-world experiences, character development, academic mindsets, and collaborative work.

The Fertile Grounds Project:
www.fertilegrounds.org

Based in New York City, this nonprofit organization reaches young people typically left behind by public school education. The Hallway Project helps at-risk high school students get on track to graduate through project based learning, and Camp Kadia teaches survival and leadership skills to inner-city youth through outdoor education.

The Coalition of Essential Schools:
www.essentialschools.org

The Coalition of Essential Schools has been at the forefront of creating and sustaining personalized, equitable, and intellectually challenging schools. Guided by a set of Common Principles, Essential Schools are places of powerful student learning where all students have the chance to reach their full potential. Diverse in size, population, and programmatic emphasis. Essential schools serve K-12 students in urban, suburban, and rural communities. You can find local schools and centers here.[37]

Institute for Democratic Education in America:
www.democraticeducation.org

The Institute for Democratic Education in America (IDEA) is a national organization that works to catalyze educational change based on democratic value and human rights. They also keep an up-to-date listing of alternatives to traditional schools.[38]

North Star Self-Directed Learning for Teens:
northstarteens.org

North Star is a small, safe, and welcoming community of learners. North Star teens are individuals, moving forward in unique direc-

---

[37] www.essentialschools.org/network.html.

[38] democraticeducation.org/index.php/library/category/C68

tions at a pace that is right for them. North Star is not a school. Rather, North Star offers an alternative to school that has been supporting teens to find and pursue their passions since 1996. Most North Star teens choose to go on to college and do so successfully.

Liberated Learners Schools:

liberatedlearners.com

Liberated Learners, Inc. supports the creation of centers based on the North Star model that promote living and learning without school. Their site includes a directory of member schools.

If an alternative high school option does not sound appealing, that's okay. The next sections will provide you with options that don't involve high school.

Options for consideration before you turn 18

If you're opting out of school, you need to know where it is you want to end up so you can start working toward getting there. Actually, you should be doing that in school too, but often there's little attention focused on that. Sure, in school you will be told to go to college, but many people never really know why they're doing this. You should know, so start thinking. You should have at least one of these options in place by the age of 18, and, ideally, before. Your ePortfolio (more on that later) will help you land an experience that is well matched to your background.

1. Become a volunteer

Volunteer work provides great experience and helps you make the world a little bit better. Find volunteer organizations in your area and see how you might be able to help. A fun way to get inspiration might be to watch the show <u>Secret Millionaire</u>.

2. Do an apprenticeship/mentorship/internship

In later sections of this guide you'll learn how to discover and pursue your passion and develop your personal learning network. As you begin to learn about what you love and connect with others who love the same thing, you may come across someone willing to have you join him or her to "learn the ropes." There is usually not much (or any!) pay in the beginning, but the payoff can be significant. Take for example Rahaf Harfoush.[39] She was interested in social media and how it could affect political campaigns. She volunteered to assist on Barack Obama's "Yes We Can!" social media campaign. Following that she wrote the book "*Yes We Did: An Insider's Look at How Social Media Built the Obama Brand,*"[40] and now tours the world speaking about a topic she is passionate about...and, as a side note, she makes a very good living!

3.   Become an entrepreneur

You are never too young to become an entrepreneur. In fact it is at the heart of the work of some alternative schools like Nuestra Escuela. What do you love to do that you're good at? Perhaps someone would like your help in doing that. Maybe you're great at downloading iTunes songs for someone who just doesn't have the time. Perhaps you love shopping and can do so for someone who hates it. Maybe

---

[39] www.rahafharfoush.com
[40] www.rahafharfoush.com/yeswedid

you're great at repairing bikes or TVs. Perhaps you are terrific at making videos. They send you the footage, you'll make magic. Do you love to cook and have people in your neighborhood who don't have time? Provide home cooked meals. Figure it out and showcase your wares to people who might be interested locally or online.

4. Get a job

If you are out of school, you'll have advantages of your schooling friends while you're making the bucks and figuring out what you like, love, and hate. Check out all this inspiration about jobs teens who didn't go to high school were able to get <u>here</u>.[41]

5. Join the military

Homeschoolers have been admitted to all of the US military academies. These government-funded institutions pay all college expenses for four years and expect terms of service upon graduation that range from 5 to 10 years. Find out more <u>here</u>[42].

---

[41] sandradodd.com/teen/jobs
[42] www.thehomeschoolmom.com/high-school-beyond/homeschool-to-military.
[42] www.huffingtonpost.com/lisa-nielsen/the-college-myth-why-coll_b_827633.html

6. **Take college classes**

As shared earlier, just because you don't go to school doesn't mean you don't have to go to college. Take classes you love. If college seems like a good fit, then a degree might be something you want to pursue

7. *Uncollege* **your learning**

In school everyone talks about how important college is. The reality is college is only the right option for those who are pursuing certain careers that now mandate college such as doctors, nurses, lawyers. For many careers, college really isn't worth the time or the cost.[43] If you want a college experience but not the cost or having someone else telling you to do work that you don't care about or just might not be that meaningful, Uncollege might be right for you. Visit the UnCollege website.[44] You may just learn a lot more than many of us learned in four years of school.

---

44 www.uncollege.org

Open Educational Resources

Open Educational Resources is a coordinated movement to provide quality courses and learning materials for free.

> *At the heart of the movement toward Open Educational Resources is the simple and powerful idea that the world's knowledge is a public good and that technology in general, and the Worldwide Web in particular, provide an extraordinary opportunity for everyone to share, use, and re-use knowledge.*
> *~ The William and Flora Hewlett Foundation*

OER lets you study whatever you select from wherever you want whenever you want. This includes full courses, modules, syllabi, lectures, homework assignments, quizzes, lab activities, pedagogical materials, games, simulations, and many more resources contained in digital media collections from around the world. You can access OER at www.oercommons.org.[45]

---

[45] www.oercommons.org

High school equivalency exam

Most people, most of the time, learn most of what they know about science and technology outside of school.
 ~ *National Science Foundation*

If a school setting isn't right for you, a high school equivalency exam such as the GED (general education development) is one practical alternative. In most states you must be 16 and the test and preparation is free.

You may have heard that a high school equivalency will result in limited career options. Not true. Historically, in fact, many careers did not require a high school or college diploma. As we've progressed through time, our society has encountered academic inflation meaning to get a job they keep increasing education requirements that never before existed. The result is that we are calling today's generation of college graduates "Generation Debt," as they walk out of schools with a diploma in hand and often haven't been prepared to pursue a career about which they are passionate.

Don't worry though. You will have time to find and learn about what you love, but first you must think about the type of career you might want to pursue and what it would require. For many careers a trade school, internship, or apprenticeship will get you on your way to becoming prepared or at least exploring what you are interested in.

If college is interests you, you can do that too. You may want to consider starting slowly, taking a class here or there about topics you are interested in. You can attend as a non-matriculated student. If you decide you want to go full time and apply for college you'll need to show you're homeschooled or you'll need your high school equivalency.

This next section will explain how to attend college without going to high school.

Attending college without going to high school
If you're thinking of opting out of high school but you still want to go to college, don't worry! A secret many are unaware of is that you don't have to go to high school to get into col-

lege. And I don't just mean community college. I mean a very good college. In fact, I don't just mean a very good college, I mean the best colleges. In fact as the Learn in Freedom[46] website explains, "Harvard College specifically mentions that they have never required a high school diploma for admission. Stanford University makes clear in a form letter to home learning applicants that a high school diploma is not necessary for admission. More and more colleges are following their lead and mentioning admission policies for home learners in their on-line or in printed materials."

Homeschoolers[47] have now matriculated at over 900 different colleges and universities, including institutions with highly selective standards of admission, such as the US military academies, Rice University, Harvard University, Stanford University, Cornell University, Brown University, Dartmouth College, and Princeton University. The Learning in Freedom[48] site pro-

---

46 learninfreedom.org
47 Wkipedia: en.wikipedia.org/wiki/Homeschooling#cite_note-18
48 learninfreedom.org/open_4_hmsc.html
9 clep.collegeboard.org

vides a list of colleges that will admit students who haven't attended school.

Another option home learning students are pursuing is earning college credit at community colleges or online before attending a traditional college. From a financial perspective it might make good sense to earn credits from a more an affordable institution in advance of attending a traditional four-year institution.

Another option is to earn college credits through standardized tests such as the College Level Examination Program[49] (CLEP). CLEP is a group of standardized tests that assess college-level knowledge in several subject areas. Students earn credit by passing the tests. Over at the College for Homeschoolers[50] site, Calfi Cohen shares additional great tips such as colleges that provide a free education for those who meet their requirements, colleges whose programs have students engaging in real world work and experiences, colleges without exams or grades, a college geared toward students with ADHD, as well as advice for those who want to

50 www.collegeforhomeschoolers.com/college_admissions.shtml

homeschool for college and attend a "virtual" university.

If you're thinking, "This sounds great, but a student who has not attended school surely must meet some admission requirements." You are right. You can see how people like, Kate Frikis and others got into college without school search "College without School" at InnovativeEducator.com where you'll find out about services like Clonlara which will help students create a transcript colleges will love. Here are things you can do to ensure you get into the school of your choice.

Prepare for college admission

Not only can you get into a good college without going to school but as the Learn in Freedom website explains, those who prepare thoroughly can even be admitted with scholarships. The site goes on to explain that colleges that accept home learners rely on various materials in place of high school grades. While criteria will vary widely, here are some of requirements schools may request:

- High School Equivalency such as GED
- Grades from open admission community colleges
- SAT or ACT scores
- Some selective colleges will admit anyone with a score above a certain level.
- This is not a requirement for all colleges. According to FairTest, the Center for Fair and Open Testing, there are more than 800 colleges and universities that no longer require the SAT for some or all applicants. Here is a <u>list of those schools</u>.[51]
- Extracurricular activities could be a key to getting a scholarship
- Personal recommendations
- Portfolios of student work
- Applicant's personal essay

The College Board, who sponsors the SAT college-entrance exams, has created a page devoted to the application process for those who have not attended school that <u>outlines the approach such students must take</u>[52] to be accepted into college.

---

51 www.fairtest.org/university/optional
52 www.collegeboard.com/student/apply/the-application/56.html

Sandra Dodd has compiled some terrific resources sharing how student work can be documented for a portfolio in her blog post[53] and on this page from her site [54] as well as how you can turn the curriculum of a home learner into "educationese" more consistent with the institutional jargon which you can see at these links.[55] Helen Barrett also has terrific information on how to create electronic/digital portfolios using free tools on her site.[56]

Passions and Portfolios
Exploring, discovering, and pursuing your passions

School is torture because I am required to spend all my time doing menial tasks, worksheets, and rote memorization. This takes too much time away from being able to discover my hobbies, interests, or passions. I'm in 10th grade and I don't foresee having the ability to do that before I graduate high school.

~ *Adam Ritter,[57] honors student*

---

53 joyful-abundance.blogspot.com/2010/06/educationese-for-beginners-and.html
54 sandradodd.com/curriculum/portfolio
55 sandradodd.com/curriculum, sandradodd.com/acme2, www.parentatthehelm.com/2053/educationese-for-beginners
56 electronicportfolios.com.
57 www.facebook.com/adam.ritter.90?fref=ts

Unfortunately, if you're not passionate about Reading, wRiting and aRithmetic taught in the standardized school-y way, you may not have had the opportunity to discover your passions, talents, and interests. That's okay! You are still young and now that you've chosen not to partake in the one-size-fits all traditional model of schooling, you'll have more time to discover what you love.

Here are some ideas to get started.

You might want to read some books about finding your passion. You can find one such collection at www.theonequestion.com/lifepurposebooks. If videos are more your style, www.thepassiontest.com has videos with experts who talk about the importance of living their passions. The I Need Motivation[58] site shares 7 simple questions you can ask yourself to discover your passion.

1. What puts a smile on your face?
1. What do you find easy?
2. What sparks your creativity?

---

58 www.ineedmotivation.com

3. What would you do for free?
4. What do you like to talk about?
5. What makes you unafraid of failure?
6. What would you regret not having tried?

There are also, fun, interactive tests you can take online like the one featured on the game tab at www.wearethepeoplemovie.com. It lets you take a test to figure out your career path. The site also has a plethora of useful information which you can access by clicking about the site where you are connected to experts, students, celebrities and others speaking about issues in education.

Myers Briggs is another popular test to help you see what passions and talents may be right for you. Here is one site where you can <u>take the test</u>[59] for free.

Discovering your passions is fun! A great way to pursue your passions is by connecting with others who share them so you can learn from and with others who have experience doing what you <u>enjoy. A terrifi</u>c way to do this is by building a

---

[59] www.quistic.com/personality-type/test

personal learning network, which is the topic of the next section.

Building your personal learning network

Personal Learning Networks are a terrific way to extend your knowledge and learning. They allow you to find, connect, and share with others that share your talents, passions, and interests. They are great vehicles for students who want to learn more about any topic. As students build relationships in these communities it could even lead to internship, mentorship and/or apprenticeship type opportunities both online and face-to-face. Here are a few ideas for getting started.

1. **Join a learning network.**
Try to find online communities where others share your passion. . Facebook, Twitter, and Google Plus are great places to start. Use the search features to find groups, pages, and posts of interest, and start following authors and speakers, and engage with replies to their posts. Online discussion boards are also use-

ful. If you don't find anything related to your topics of interest, consider creating your own groups.

1. Read Blogs

Once you have some interests in mind, reading blogs is a great way to get up-to-date information.

2. Subscribe to your blogs with Feedly

Feedly provides a great way for you to follow the blogs in which you are interested. Visit Feedly[60] and add the blogs you want to follow or look at blogs in various topics of interest. Caution: Try to limit the number of blogs you follow or it could become overwhelming.

3. Start Commenting

Become a part of the conversation and start commenting on the blogs you read. This will enable you to get to know the blog author and readers. Share your thoughts, ideas, and ask questions. Blogging finally puts people in touch with experts in areas of passion, talents,

---

60 feedly.com

and interests. If you have something more to offer, perhaps you can request contributing a guest post.

4. **Become Twitterate!**

Tweeting to learn may not be the most common use of Twitter among school age youth, but it should be! Twitter is an untapped adolescence treasure trove of potential experts and others who care about what you care about.

You can start by searching #unschool or #homeschool into a Twitter search. Connected to many other people who share that interest. See what they're saying. If they say something you like, "follow" them. You will quickly get to know who the experts are in the topics you care about. They become a great resource for you. If you mention one of the experts when you Tweet, this will show up in their feed and you are likely to get a response. It has never been easier to connect with other people who share your interests.

5. YouTube

Not only is YouTube one of the Internet's primary sources of learning, it is also a place where you can solicit help from others about things you want to know! To learn something, just type in the search. If you can find something to comment on, you should. This helps you build relationships with others who share your interests. You might also use YouTube to solicit help in doing something you want to know more about. That's what one young man who goes by the name of bushkrafft[61] on YouTube did when he needed help with his bow drill set.[62] Just make your video, share it with your personal learning network and connect with others from whom you can learn.

6. Skype

Integrating Skype into your personal learning network is powerful! Simply connect with someone who shares your interest and ask him or her to talk or teach via Skype. This, in essence, turns your bedroom, living room, or wherever you are connecting into a global

61 www.youtube.com/user/bushkrafft
62 www.youtube.com/watch?v=JuFsDN8dsJU
63 weblogg-ed.com/2007/supplementing-my-kids-education/

communication center. Author, blog-evangelist, teacher, thought leader, and father Will Richardson uses Skype to <u>supplement his children's learning</u>[63] by sending out Tweets using smart hashtagging and mentioning what his children are interested in learning more about then schedules a time for a Skype learning session. Paul Bogush, an 8th grade social studies teacher, supports his students in using Skype to produce called Lunchtime Leaders where students interview leaders from around the world on their opinions about what they should do to be prepared for the future. Bogush and his students do their interviews using Skype, and they turn the interviews into podcasts. Anyone can put together a show using Skype and invite smart people to share and discuss ideas. When those ideas are published even more people have the opportunity to learn and connect with you.

So get to it and start building your learning network. Join a learning network, subscribe to blogs, comment on YouTube, Skype and Tweet.

Start with one and move to the next. When you do, you are likely to find you learned a lot more than you ever learned in class.

Creating a personal success plan

Study without desire spoils the memory, and it retains nothing that it takes in.

~ *Leonardo da Vinci*

Though people are very different, each with their own passions, talents, interests, and abilities, in traditional school settings, students are all given the same path and grouped with others by date of manufacture. At the age where youth are entering college or the workforce, many have never been given the opportunity to find what they love. This is because for many students, school fosters dependency-learning and a false sense that if you just keep doing as you're told, it will eventually pay off...even though there may never be time to figure out where it is you actually want to go.

This holds true not only for students dissatisfied with school, but also for students with high achievement like Erica Goldson, the insightful Valedictorian who felt high school robbed her of the opportunity to discover what she loved. Upon graduation, she took her diploma and literally hit the road to make up for lost time and explore who she really is and what she loves. You can follow her adventures on her blog <u>America Via Erica</u>[64]. You'll notice that once she left school behind, Erica had the opportunity to set her own personal goals, which she can change and update as she learns and as she pleases. In her blog she states her goals are:

- attend survival course
- buy survival gear
- buy a van
- learn Korean
- avoid arrest

Making goals for personal success is something that is often overlooked in school. Schools attempt to define your goals for you:

- Go to school

---

[64] americaviaerica.blogspot.com

- Take tests and hand in papers
- Get good grades
- Do as your told and stay out of trouble
- Don't socialize unless you are given permission
- Get into college even if you have no idea of your passions, talents, and interests

Now that you have made the decision to leave school you get to determine your own goals and a plan for achieving them! It's probably a good idea to start this plan before you leave school, as it is something that will demonstrate to yourself and others that you know what you want and you have a plan for achieving it. At PersonalDevelopment.com they suggest there are key points that will help you achieve the highest levels of success (read the full article here.[65])

1. Look into the nearest mirror.
1. Smile back at your reflection.
2. Positive self-esteem is the foundation for success.
3. Believe in yourself.

---

65 www.personal-development.com/articles/12point.htm

4. Desire to be a success.
5. Associate with successful people.
6. Avoid unsuccessful people.
7. Do what you are best at and that which gives you the most satisfaction.
8. Write down a vision of how you want to live your life.
9. Write down you biggest goal, the one you most want to fulfill.
10. Study the science of success.
11. Every day do something that brings you closer to your goal.

These are great points to keep in mind, but how will you bring your plan to life? Joe Renzulli and Sally Reiss, who developed the Schoolwide Enrichment Model, have also developed a great system for determining and tracking your personal success. It's aptly named "The Personal Success Plan" and it has two main objectives.

1. Provide a research-based, goal-oriented assessment and treatment tool that establishes student ownership of the value of his/her education.
2. Support students in their identification and pursuit of social, academic, and ultimately economic short & long-term goals.

The plan has the following components:

- <u>**My Interests**</u>

Carefully consider your **interests and talents**. Think about how those strengths connect to careers and future plans.

- <u>**My Heroes and Helpers**</u>

Heroes and Helpers are people that inspire you, either the heroes who may be famous and/or helpers in your own life who you may know personally.

- <u>**My Careers**</u>

You can learn about **Careers** based on your interests and begin thinking about the type of work you might want to pursue.

- <u>**My Goals**</u>

Identify long and short term academic and social/personal goals to help set priorities about what you want to accomplish in work and life.

- <u>**My Plans**</u>

Create **plans** with concrete steps, activities, and timelines to achieve future goals.

- **My Projects**

Complete creative autobiographical projects to help consider interests, role models, and careers.

Once you come up with your plan. You'll need a place to capture all the great things you are doing. This next section will help you do just that.

Developing an ePortfolio

Did you ever feel frustrated that in school you are supposed to spend all this time studying, taking tests, completing worksheets and handing in reports with no audience beyond the teacher, then, after years of that, all you're left with is a pile of tests and papers nobody cares about? School shouldn't be preparing you for more school. It should be preparing students for the world, but unfortunately, the thing that is most important often falls through the cracks and is replaced by more and more testing and measuring. If you've decided to opt out of school and into the real world, you'll have time to begin preparing your ePortfolio where you can share with everyone the wonderful work you are doing!

In the real world, ePortfolios are actually just called websites or blogs and the point is to show the world how fabulous you are and what you can do. When you create it here are some of the sections you may consider including.

- **Landing page**:

This is the main page and gives your audience an overview of who you are and what you do.

- **About Me page**:

Give a brief overview of yourself and your talents. You may want this page to have links to pictures of you as well as your resume.

- **What People Are Saying**:

You may want to collect and share what people are saying about you and your work.

- **Work Samples**:

Share samples of your work. You might consider organizing this by types of work or how the work is displayed i.e. photos, videos, animations, podcasts, etc.

- **Contact**:

Give people a way to contact you i.e. your email, your Facebook page, your Twitter handle.

These are some general sections that most people in the real world have. When creating your own, check out the sites of experts who share your interests and follow their lead in the parts you like.

Creating your ePortfolio aka Website or Blog

The first thing you want to do is get a domain name. One way to do this is via Google Sites which are free and easy to use. The domain name will cost you about $10 a year. Here is a guide to starting with free Google Sites[66]. If you want to make your ePortfolio more business/entrepreneurial just look at sites of those you want to be like. If you want it more education focused visit Helen Barrett's ePortfolio site at electronicportfolios.com.[67]

---

66 www.google.com/sites/overview.html
66 electronicportfolios.com

Congratulations!

You have taken responsibility to own your learning and take it seriously. Going to high school is the path for many and it may well be the path for you, but there are alternatives. You are now armed with some information toward helping you make your decision. Now it is up to you, and your parents, to decide if *the road less traveled* may make sense in your endeavors toward achieving your personal plans for success.

About the Author and Contributors

About the author

Lisa Nielsen

Lisa Nielsen, The Innovative Educator, works in New York City where she enjoys helping to support students in the acquisition of learning in innovative, real and relevant ways. As a student Lisa received good grades, but spent most of high school sleeping in classes that bored her or day dreaming about how to get out of the boring prison known as school. She couldn't wait to be done with high school and college so she could see why and how she could finally apply all these things she was told she needed to know to real life. At 19 she found herself with a college diploma in one hand and with the other she was scratching her head. She had boxes of tests and papers, a high G.P.A. but no idea what she might want to do next and no one had ever asked. She was duped! As a result she went in the field of education to do her best to ensure future students have the opportunity to receive more relevant and meaningful educational experiences with opportunities for real work and the opportunity to discover and develop passions.

Lisa invites you to follow her blog at Innovative Educator.com, follow her on Twitter @InnovativeEdu and read her book, Teaching Generation Text, which you can find on her blog.

About the contributors

Deven Black

Deven Black is, paradoxically, a public school teacher trained in library sciences and special education who is opposed to schooling. He works in New York City. He opted out of high school, gave it one more try, opted out again, started college and opted out of that, all before he was 17. Somewhere in the middle of successful careers in newspapers, radio news and restaurant management (among other things) he finally found a college that met his criteria and got a BS at age 43. Six years later, tired of restaurant management and looking for something else to do, his son's elementary school principal suggested he try substitute teaching. It was magic. Deven signed up at a prestigious university where he got a vacuous MS degree and became a full-time teacher at age 50. He also received a second MS as a teacher librarian. He is still waiting for graduate school to teach him something useful that he doesn't already know.

You can follow him at educationontheplate.wordpress.com and on Twitter @devenkblack.

Amanda Enclade & Erick Brownstein

Amanda Enclade and Erick Brownstein are the parents of 3 unschooled boys. Obsessed with shifting traditional educational paradigms and creating alternatives, their unschooling journey began in 2007 when their oldest son opted out of public high school in early tenth grade. Like modern day Johnny Appleseeds, they are planting seeds of possibility, sharing their experiences with the challenges and rewards of pursuing alternative learning paths. Amanda is a far out thinker, non-conformist, foodie, lover, inventor, blogger, aromatherapist, magic mixer and healer of every day things. Erick is an aspiring expert at nothing and recovering overachiever smarty pants.

You can follow Amanda at amandaenclade.blogspot.com and on Twitter @aenclade. She also shares her magical healing products at auntvis.com. Erick works as a creative, social strategist and blogs at thenewagency.com/blog and tweets @ErickB.

Laurette Lynn

Laurette Lynn is an author, blogger, media broadcaster, and a homeschooling Mom of three. In her work, Laurette covers a range of sociopolitical topics relevant to personal independence. Her presentations, have reached and inspired thousands. Through her training and classes, Laurette helps bolster and improve presentation and communication skills to those who want to reach, motivate, educate, inform and inspire their networks and community more effectively.

An independently educating Mother who unplugged from schooling herself, Laurette emphasizes the need to disconnect our perspective from the notion of 'schooling' in order to reconnect to the natural world where spiritual, emotional and physical health await. Laurette dives into this in her book, Don't Do Drugs and

Stay Out of School (www.unpluggedmom.com/book).

You can follow Laurette at www.laurettelynn.com and on Twitter @TheLaurettteLynn.

Leah Miller

Leah left high school halfway through sophomore year, and now she enjoys her life and learns from everything around her, not in hour-long periods of enforced learning. Her passion is musical theater and she breathes it everyday. She is on a quest to find a better term than "unschooling". Leah enjoys mismatched socks, driving with the windows open and the music blasting, and baking. She would be very content to never hear the words, "So what do you do all day?" ever again.

Leah writes a blog called "said the red-head" (leahmiller.typepad.com) and you can also follow her on twitter @LeahMiller28.

www.ingramcontent.com/pod-product-compliance
Lightning Source LLC
Chambersburg PA
CBHW070155080526
44586CB00015B/1996